BRIGHT · SPARKS

Patterns in nature

by
Rosie Dalzell

Photographs: Zul Mukhida

Series Consultant: Sue Dale Tunnicliffe

CHERRYTREE BOOKS

A Cherrytree Book

Devised and produced by
Touchstone Publishing Ltd,
68 Florence Road, Brighton,
East Sussex BN1 6DJ

First published 1992
by Cherrytree Press Ltd
a subsidiary of
The Chivers Company Ltd,
Windsor Bridge Road,
Bath, Avon BA2 3AX

British Library Cataloguing in Publication data
Dalzell, Rosemary
  Patterns in nature. - (Bright sparks)
  I. Title II. Series
  574

  ISBN 0-7451-5140-X

Printed and bound by
Proost N.V., Turnhout, Belgium

Contents

Projects

Words

Difficult words are explained on page 26.

Check

Before you start any project, check to see if there is a safety note (marked **!**) in the text. This means you need an adult to help you.

Snail trails

How do snails walk? Do they have feet? Collect some from under stones in damp places. Watch them move on a sheet of paper. Look for their trails of sticky **mucus**.

Lawrence is sandpapering some chalk dust on to a piece of paper. The dust sticks to mucus. Later he can shake the paper and see the pattern of the snail trails.

Emily is tilting her shelf. Will the snails fall off? Try this with your snails. Be very gentle with them.

◀ **Look underneath a snail moving on a see-through surface. Can you see how its muscles are working?**

Tree shapes

One winter day, go outside and look for trees. Each kind of tree has a special shape, but some trees can't grow into their true shape. Can you see why?

Look for trees with clear shapes and draw them in a notebook. Do they have leaves, or berries or interesting bark? Mark all the things you notice about the trees.

Gareth is cutting out his tree shapes and writing their names on the back. Find out the names of the trees you have drawn and make your own stand-up forest.

◀ **The tall tree on the left is an** evergreen.

▶**The one on the right loses all its leaves in winter.**

Petal patterns

Pick a flower and look at it closely. Gently pull off the **petals**. How many are there? Can you see the **sepals**?

Lawrence is dusting the pollen at the end of a **stamen** on to a piece of paper. Find the stamens in your flower. What colour is the pollen? Now feel the **stigma** in the centre of your flower. Is it sticky?

Arrange the parts of your flower on blotting paper, as Emily is doing. To keep your pattern, put paper on top and press it in a flower press or inside a thick book.

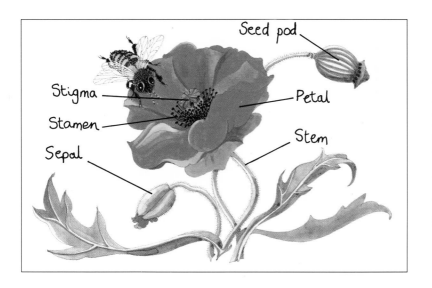

◄ **Bees carry pollen from one poppy flower to another. Pollen sticks to the stigma so poppy seeds can grow.**

Seed propellers

Plants scatter their seeds to give them room to grow.
Look at the seeds in the picture. How do they travel?

Kate has made models of sycamore seeds with card and
clay. Now she is testing them to see how they fly. Leila
is using wire and tissue paper to make an ash seed.
Will it fly through the air in the same way as Kate's
seed?

Make some model seeds with wings, or **parachutes**.
Copy the real ones carefully and find out how they fly.

▶ **These winged seeds are
sycamore and ash.
Dandelion seeds have
parachutes, and clematis
seeds have feathery tails.**

Leaf pictures

Rachel has been collecting leaves and pressing them between the pages of a book. She is making a pattern to show the colours of some of the leaves.

Look for interesting leaves outside. Sort them out into different shapes. Which trees have narrow leaves, like needles? Can you find round leaves, heart-shaped leaves, and hand-shaped leaves with five points?

Try making a picture or pattern with your leaves.

◀ **An artist made this** sculpture **by placing leaves in a pattern on the ground.**

Seeds and fruits

Collect as many different seeds as you can. Which ones are good to eat? Which ones need cooking first?

Sometimes it is the **fruit** around the seeds that we eat. Cut open some fruits you like to eat. How are the seeds packed inside? How many seeds are there in each fruit?

Press out a flat shape of coloured playdough on greaseproof paper or a plate. Make a pattern of the seeds you collected to show their shapes and colours.

! **Ask an adult what seeds you may eat.**

▶ **The seeds of most plants grow inside the fruit. Do we eat the seeds or the fruit of these 'vegetables'?**

Go mouldy!

Emily is dropping water in a pattern on fresh bread. Then she will leave it, sealed in a jar, until mould grows. Where will it grow first, on the wet or dry bread? Would it grow faster in a hot place or in a fridge?

Try Emily's experiment and find out. Put the bread in two sealed jars. Make a hole in each lid and tape cotton wool over it. Leave the jars in different places and see what happens. Grow mould on some other foods in jars.

! Do not open the jars or touch the mould. Ask an adult to help you empty your jars.

◀ **A mould is a** fungus **that feeds on plants or animals or foods made from them. This bracket fungus lives on trees.**

Grow a pattern

Leila is sowing seeds in a window box. Next she will sprinkle soil on top and wait for shoots to appear. What else will the seeds need to make them grow?

Grow your own box garden. Plant seeds in a special pattern. Will you sow flowers or vegetables? Find a sunny spot for the box. Which way do the shoots point? Turn the box round for a few days. What happens?

Kate's vegetable garden is growing very well. Why is she pulling out some **seedlings** now?

▶ **To make this clock pattern, the gardener sowed seeds in boxes. Later he planted out the young plants.**

Disappearing dinosaurs

Most animals need to be able to hide. Why? Think of animals whose colours and markings help them hide. Are their coats or skins one colour or are they patterned?

Paint a place where dinosaurs might have lived. Then choose colours for a cut-out dinosaur so that it disappears into its background. No one knows what colours dinosaurs really were, so you may be right!

Rachel's dinosaurs are striped and spotted. Would plain colours blend in better? Try it and see.

◀ **Fallow deer have spotted coats in summer to hide them in dappled light under trees. This is called** camouflage.

Mirror magic

How much of Kate can you see? Where is the rest of her? Tom's mirror makes a line of **symmetry**. It divides her in two. One half is the same as the other.

Is Leila's flower symmetrical? Could she divide her flower another way to get identical halves? How many ways could she divide it? Get a mirror and a flower and see how many lines of symmetry you can find.

Look at other living things. How many ways can you divide them into mirror-image halves?

! **Be very careful not to break the mirror and cut yourself.**

▶ **Most animals have only one line of symmetry. But how many has this starfish?**

Butterfly frighteners

Instead of trying to hide, some animals frighten or trick their enemies. Rachel is designing butterflies to surprise the birds. Why has she put circles and spots like eyes on their wings?

Invent your own frightening butterfly. Fold a piece of paper in half. Unfold it and paint half the butterfly on one side of the fold. Use bright colours and lots of paint.

Then fold your paper again and press the two halves together. Open it slowly. Are you surprised?

◀ **A peacock butterfly can open its wings to flash two eye-spots at an enemy.**

Words to remember

Camouflage A disguise to hide something so that it disappears into the background.

Evergreen A tree that has green leaves all year round.

Fruit The part of a plant that contains the seeds.

Fungus A living thing that is not green, feeds on plants and animals, and does not move. Both moulds and mushrooms are kinds of fungus.

Mucus A sticky or slippery substance produced by an animal. We have mucus in our noses.

Parachute Something which is used to slow down a fall through air. Parachutes are often umbrella-shaped.

Petal The outer, coloured part of a flower.

Sculpture The art of shaping objects or statues from stone, wood, metal or any other material.

Seedlings Very young plants.

Sepal The part of a flower that protects the flower bud.

Stamen The male part of a flower with pollen on the end.

Stigma The outside of the female part of a flower.

Symmetry When an object has exactly the same shape on each side of an imaginary dividing line, or line of symmetry.

Books for you

My First Nature Book by Angela Wilkes (Dorling Kindersley)
Animals and Plants by Hannah Glease (Cherrytree)
Hide and Seek and *Animals Showing Off* pop-up books
(National Geographic Society)

Books to look at with an adult

Trees in Britain and *Wild Flowers of Britain* by Roger
Phillips (Pan)
Mysteries and Marvels of Nature by Rick Morris and Barbara
Cook (Usborne)
Living Things by Sue Dale Tunnicliffe (Think and Do Cards,
Basil Blackwell)

Places to go

The Discovery Centre, Whipsnade Wild Animal Park,
Dunstable, Bedfordshire LU6 2LF. Animals, their lives and
habitats. *London Zoo* also has a discovery centre.
Natural History Museum, Cromwell Road, London SW7 5BD.
Edinburgh Zoo, Murrayfield, Edinburgh EH12 6TS.
Northern Ireland Aquarium, Rope Walk, Portaferry
BT22 1NZ. Local sea life, touch tank and ecology display.
Cardigan Wildlife Park, Cardigan, Dyfed SA43 2BT.

More sparky ideas

Here are some background facts, things to look out for and ideas for more experiments.

pp 4-5 Snail trails
● A snail has a single muscular foot which stretches and contracts to pull it forwards.
● A film of mucus from a gland under its head helps the snail to glide along and gives good suction for climbing. Snails can carry fifty times their own weight.
● The two larger tentacles have eyes at the end, which can only see light and dark. The smaller tentacles are for tasting and smelling. Usually, snails indoors move in roughly the same direction, away from light.

pp 6-7 Tree shapes
● A tree may be misshapen because it is in a windy position or is crowded and has to compete with other plants for light, or because it has been lopped. Age may also affect its shape.
● Take notes about where each tree is growing. Make bark rubbings using soft crayon on strong paper to help identify your trees.
● Keep budding twigs of a deciduous tree in water indoors and watch the leaves gradually appear.

pp 8-9 Petal patterns
● Plants that rely on insects to carry pollen from one plant to another often have flowers that are scented or have coloured petals, shaped or marked to help guide insects to the nectar inside. Some plants have both.
● In contrast, the flowers of wind-pollinated plants, such as grasses and conifers, are small and dull.

● Once pollen grains have reached the stigma, the female part of the flower, the ovary underneath ripens to become a fruit containing seeds.

pp 10-11 Seed propellers
● The wings on a sycamore seed are set at a slight angle to give a 'twin-screw' effect which helps the seeds to spin as they fly, travelling up to 200 metres before landing.
● Seeds can be dispersed by animals, which may eat but not digest them or may carry them hooked to their fur.

pp 12-13 Leaf pictures
● Leaf shapes and colours help to identify trees. Conifers have needles or scale-like leaves. Leaves of deciduous trees range from simple, narrow willow leaves to complex compound leaves with two rows of leaflets.
● Put paper over a leaf and rub on it with a wax crayon to record its shape and vein structure.

pp 14-15 Seeds and fruits
● A fruit is a ripened ovary, a package for the seeds. Many foods that we call vegetables are really fruits.
● Humans depend heavily on seeds like corn and rice for food. Pea and bean seeds are rich sources of protein.
● Plants tempt animals to spread their seeds by packaging them in edible fruits.

pp 16-17 Go mouldy!
● Fungi grow best in damp, warm conditions. They live on other organisms so they need no light to help them make food. They are neither plants nor animals.
● Plants and animals can be damaged or even killed by fungi, but some fungi are useful as food (mushrooms) and in wine-making and baking (yeasts). Fungi help the breakdown of dead plants and animals in the soil.

● The blue and green mould on lemons is *Penicillium*. A similar mould makes the natural antibiotic penicillin and is also used to make blue cheeses.

pp 18-19 Grow a pattern
● Green plants need warmth, sunlight and water to grow. Indoors, the shoots grow towards the daylight; outside, they grow towards the sun. The seedlings usually need thinning out later.
● Vegetables are easy to grow. Lettuces, spring onions and radishes all mature quickly. The plants in the picture are nasturtiums, marigolds, alyssum and stocks.

pp 20-21 Disappearing dinosaurs
● An animal's camouflage enables it to stalk its food unseen and avoid being eaten. Polar bears and tabby cats can creep up on their prey. Caterpillars can't easily be seen on leaves; nor can plaice on a pebbly sea-bed.
● We use colour to hide, too. Soldiers' uniforms are in mottled colours to blend in with their surroundings.

pp 22-23 Mirror magic
● Most animals have only one line of symmetry, but starfish have five, and sea urchins about twenty. An arrangement of parts spreading out from a central point is called radial symmetry.
● Many flowers are radially symmetrical, like both the pressed flowers in the picture. Leila's has eight petals and sixteen lines of symmetry.

pp 24-25 Butterfly frighteners
● When they are in danger, some toads and snakes roll over, displaying spotted, brightly coloured bellies. The puss-moth caterpillar has large, eye-like markings and the false-eyed frog even has eye-spots on its bottom.

Index

Thank you!

The author and publishers would like to thank junior scientists Alice, Ben, Charlie, Christopher, Emily, Francesca, Joanna, Maxim and Oliver for their work on the experiments; and Lawrence, Emily, Gareth, Kate, Rachel and Leila for appearing in the photographs.

Thanks also to the staff of St Bartholomew's CE First School, Knoll Infants School, Queens Park First School and Balfour First School, all of Brighton and Hove, for their co-operation.

The author would also like to thank Hilary Osborne and Dr Peter Morden of The Natural History Museum for giving so willingly of their time and expertise, and Hugh, Thomas, Kate and Harry for all their help and encouragement.

Credits

The projects were devised and set up by the author. The studio photographs are by Zul Mukhida, with backgrounds by Maureen Jackson. Other pictures were supplied by: Eye Ubiquitous (Yiorgos Nikiteas), p. 6 left; Eye Ubiquitous (Neil Campbell-Sharp), p. 6 right; Eye Ubiquitous (V.C. Sievey), p. 16; Andy Goldsworthy, p. 12; ZEFA (Shostal), p. 20; ZEFA (Dr Sauer), p. 22; ZEFA (Brockhaus), p. 24; Zul Picture Library, p. 18.

The illustration on p. 8 is by Maggie Brand.